*Children's Guide
to Parents
& Other Matters*

CHILDREN'S GUIDE TO PARENTS & OTHER MATTERS

Little Essays for Children & Others

By ELI SIEGEL

*With an Introduction by Ellen Reiss
& Drawings by Dorothy Koppelman*

DEFINITION PRESS   NEW YORK

Definition Press, New York 10012

©1971 by Eli Siegel
New Introduction and Drawings ©2003 by Definition Press

All rights reserved. No part of this book may be reproduced or transmitted in any form or by any means, electronic or mechanical, including photocopying, recording, or by any information storage and retrieval system, without permission in writing from the Publisher. For information regarding permission, write to Definition Press, 141 Greene Street, New York, NY 10012.

First published 1971

Reprinted 2003, with a new introduction by Ellen Reiss
and additional drawings by Dorothy Koppelman

Library of Congress Cataloging-in-Publication Data

Siegel, Eli, 1902-1978
Children's guide to parents and other matters: little essays for children and others.
    p.   cm.
1. Aesthetic Realism. 2. Parents. 3. Friendship. 4. Reading.
5. Anger. 6. Love. 7. Money—its meaning. 8. Beauty.
I. Koppelman, Dorothy. II. Reiss, Ellen. III. Title.

PS3537 .I295 C5
814'5'4   78-171393
ISBN 0-910492-16-6

Printed in the United States of America on acid-free paper

CONTENTS

INTRODUCTION by Ellen Reiss   7

From the PROLOGUE TO THE 1971 EDITION   11

  1. CARING FOR SOMEBODY   17

  2. ABOUT BEAUTIFUL THINGS   22

  3. PEOPLE   30

  4. MOTHERS   37
      and BIG QUESTIONS FOR LITTLE ONES   43

  5. ABOUT MONEY   45

  6. OBJECTS   50

  7. FEELING BAD   53

  8. HAPPENINGS   58

  9. BEING ANGRY   62

10. WORK   70

11. BOOKS   75

12. THE WORLD   81

INTRODUCTION

Eli Siegel wrote the Little Essays for Children in 1945, and they have met children's hopes all these years. They meet a child's hope that what goes on inside him or her be really understood. They meet a child's hope that the big, often confusing world around him or her can really have sense made of it—and be a friend.

These essays are lively and deep and surprising and beautifully logical. Their author is the American poet, educator, and critic who founded the philosophy Aesthetic Realism; and the following principles of Aesthetic Realism stated by him are at the basis of this book:

1. The deepest desire of every person is to like the world on an honest or accurate basis.

2. The greatest danger for a person is to have contempt for the world and what is in it....Contempt can be defined as the lessening of what is different from oneself as a means of self-increase as one sees it.

3. All beauty is a making one of opposites, and the making one of opposites is what we are going after in ourselves.

Children's Guide to Parents and Other Matters is the kindest book for children I have ever read. It is a classic, with such other children's classics as Robert Louis Stevenson's *A Child's Garden of Verses,* Lewis Carroll's *Alice in Wonderland,* the best of *Mother Goose.* But this book is about life as a child meets and lives it every day. It is the text used in the loved "Learning to Like the World" class for children that is now taught at the Aesthetic Realism Foundation by Aesthetic Realism consultants Barbara Allen and Robert Murphy.

Mr. Siegel's writing in the *Children's Guide* has such respect for the mind of a child; in its clarity, it is never the least bit patronizing. This educator, whose scholarship was tremendous—who was at ease, for example, amid the subtleties and intricacies of Kant, whose knowledge of Shakespeare was thorough and whose comprehension of him was new and great—this educator, Eli Siegel, could write in a way children understood and loved. And his respect for a child's thought was evident and beautiful as he *spoke* to children too.

I know this because not only did I hear Mr. Siegel speak to children in Aesthetic Realism lessons—I had the good fortune to be such a child. With my parents, I had Aesthetic Realism lessons taught by him. And beginning at the age of four, I saw in him something people don't expect to see in anyone, yet long for: I saw, as a watchful, keen child and adult, that Eli Siegel was completely honest, entirely sincere.

It is a terrible thing that many people, including people of the press, were angry at Mr. Siegel because he was so honest and knew so much. Every child and adult who reads this book will feel how shameful that anger is, how utterly wrong and unnecessary.

I am going to quote from a lesson I had when I was nearly seven years old, to show the author of the *Children's Guide* speaking to a particular child. The subject was that of the second Little Essay, "About Beautiful Things." My source is my mother's notes, and not every answer of mine was taken down. But in what we have of this interchange, one can see Mr. Siegel gracefully, clearly, showing a child something very big, something persons for centuries have tried to understand: what beauty is—and what it had to do with *her*. He asked me, "Why do you like music?" And I answered, "Because I think it's nice." Then, in Irene Reiss's notes, there is this:

> *Eli Siegel.* Do you want to be like music?
>
> *Ellen Reiss.* What do you mean, "like music"?
>
> ES. If people know how to conduct themselves they can be like music. Do you like any particular tune?
>
> ER. I like "When You Are in Love."
>
> ES. Do you think that tune goes up and down?...Is it thin and also thick?...Do you think the notes change?

ER. Yes.

ES. I like the "St. Louis Blues" very much. The notes change but they are all about one thing. When notes do different things and they surprise you, and you think it's natural, then you have something like beauty.

The things that make for beauty, not only in music but in pictures and writing and talking, are the things that people want.

Do you think there's music in words too?—Murmur and shout?

ER. Yes.

ES. There's music in words and there's music in sound. Melody can teach you how to rise and fall and see that you are the same person.

In the last of the essays in this book, Mr. Siegel tells the little boy he addresses, James, who is every boy and girl: "The world is your partner, whatever your mind may do." That is what I love him for enabling me to see, and what this book enables children to see: The world is not something to hide from, fool, and hate. The world, with all its puzzlingness, with all its good and bad, is deeply our partner—something we can like knowing, something that excitingly and truly adds to us.

ELLEN REISS
CLASS CHAIRMAN OF AESTHETIC REALISM

New York, 2003

From the *PROLOGUE TO THE 1971 EDITION*

What is in this book is exemplified or illustrated in two passages from Wordsworth. The first is from perhaps—all in all—the greatest poem in English, if not in all languages, about children, Ode on Intimations of Immortality from Recollections of Early Childhood (published 1807). The first passage is:

> Thou, whose exterior semblance doth belie
> Thy Soul's immensity.

These two lines make lively the Aesthetic Realism belief that the whole world is present in every child, infant, toddler. If the whole world, using a mother, is the cause of a child, then that cause, in keeping with the logic of reality, is in the child. What is more, the child can feel it; and the mother can, too.

The second passage from Wordsworth telling of the deepest life of a child is from the First Book of *The Prelude*.

12 *Children's Guide*

These are the lines:

> Dust as we are, the immortal spirit grows
> Like harmony in music; there is a dark
> Inscrutable workmanship that reconciles
> Discordant elements, makes them cling together
> In one society.

In these lines, one can find the Aesthetic Realism idea that opposites are in motion in a person and are trying to be friendly; to be reconciled; or—as is said in the Aesthetic Realism publication *Is Beauty the Making One of Opposites?*—are trying to be one. One can see in a child the desire to make a one of praise of himself and doubt of himself, of praise of his mother and questioning of her, of like for the world and fear of it, of interest in the world and the making less of it. Opposites are working in a child, looking for their true relation, as sea and shore do, dark and light, curve and angle.

...We think it is right to mention that poems commenting on the *Children's Guide* are in *Hot Afternoons Have Been in Montana: Poems* and *Hail, American Development*—by the author of these prose essays. In *Hot Afternoons* are: Dear Birds, Tell This to Mothers; Twenty-one Distichs about Children; One Question;

Baskets: Their Due; Night in 1242; One of the Saddest Things in the World; Alfred-Seeable Philadelphia Sky; Quiet, Tears, Babies; All the Smoke; Poem for Ellen; Poem to a Cat; The Proud Turtle. In *Hail, American Development* are: Hell, What Is This About, Asked Again; Approaches; Song of the Potter: Ceylon Folk Poem; Little Cube in Space; Stillness in the Field; The Greatest Chinese Name in the World; The Stars That Summer; To a Slushy Pear. And there are others.

*Children's Guide
to Parents
& Other Matters*

1. CARING FOR SOMEBODY

When you, James, were born, you already had much to do with two people, your father and mother. Your father and mother, Henry and Dora, had to do with other people; so you, in a way, had to do with them, too. Now when you have to do with people, you can have an opinion about them: in fact, you can be said to have met people *by* having an opinion about them.

Now an opinion has pain or pleasure in it. All opinions do. So if you have to do with people, you have either pain or pleasure about them, or both.

If you care for somebody, you have a certain kind of pleasure, and you may have a certain kind of pain about that somebody. Let's say that a year ago (you are now eight) you met a little girl who was then six. She made

you either want to go away from her or want to be where she was; and maybe in one day, too, both. If you cared for her, she pleased you. The question is why she pleased you.

She could please you for two reasons. One, Cora, age six years, could tell you things about what everything was, make you feel new things, make you like her smile, and the way she walked, and even the way her body looked: her eyes, her hair, her feet, her hands, and things like that. Cora would then make you like her because you saw what she was and liked that, and because through her you'd come to know more about everything. She could make you feel in ways you couldn't feel all by yourself. She would tell you about what she saw—for instance, she was in Chicago at the age of four and she made Chicago come closer to you. And when she said something about a cat, maybe you saw the cat in a bigger way than if she had not told you what she thought about it. In other words, James Nash liked Cora Hill because of what Cora Hill was and what she could have James Nash feel in new ways. Cora Hill was making, just by being Cora Hill, James Nash more James Nash. This is very nice. I have nothing against it; you shouldn't have; and no philosopher should. If that was the whole story, you'd really be caring for Cora Hill.

But it wasn't the whole story, James. You liked Cora Hill's smile; you felt good sometimes when you saw her smile at something really funny or pleasant. But do you remember, James, you once wanted to make her cry, just because you felt you'd be so big if you could make her cry? And maybe you don't know this, but you also felt that if you made her cry, that would show she cared for you and had to think about you. And then, James, when she told you about the lake near Chicago and the time she went in a big boat on that lake, and the way her brother, who was also on the boat, made music on the water and got into the papers—you just didn't have a good time listening to this. You said, "Look, this

little girl, she's smaller than me; she was in Chicago and was in a big boat on the water; and had a brother who got into the papers because he played music on the water—why couldn't I have been in Chicago on the water and have a brother who got into the papers? What's all this about, anyway?"

And then when your mother asked a question once and Cora knew the answer and you didn't, you also felt bad; because you said that if you didn't know something, Cora had no right to know it, either.

And then you once made Cora go into a store with you, because you said you'd feel so bad if she didn't; and you also would have said, if you had to, that if she didn't go into the candy store with you in the next block, you wouldn't talk to her anymore. When Cora did go into the store with you, you said to yourself—do you know this?—"I can make this little girl who thinks she's so smart, do what I want her to do, and that's all there is to it."

Now when you did all these things I've just told you about, you weren't really caring for somebody. You were using somebody to care for yourself in a bad way. When you care for somebody, you feel, James, that in knowing what that somebody is, you're already happy and you can be happier in making that person more and more what she can be by showing yourself, just as you are, and at the right time.

When you care for somebody, James, you're happy that this person is alive, and you're happy to show your happiness; and you want what that person is to be more and more you; and what you are to be more and more that person; and at the same time, you want to be fair to every other person and every other thing and not to forget about them. In fact, at this time, James, you care for other people more, because you care for one person you can see by herself.

2. ABOUT BEAUTIFUL THINGS

Beauty is a hard subject; but just because it's hard, it doesn't mean you don't have to think about it. James, in my opinion, if you don't think about beauty at some time or other, you won't know, the way you want to, the reason you were born.

Take a beautiful thing: say, a song. When you hear a pretty and a good song, you are hearing many things called notes. You may also hear words. Now these notes and these words are different. Things have to be different, otherwise they wouldn't be separate things.

If you, James, hear a lot of different things, and all that you feel is that they're different, you won't have such a good time. Because your mind will be jumping from one new thing to another; and minds don't like that. Suppose you went from a butterfly to a clothespin to a person to an onion to an onion skin to a book to a cat, and each time you went to a new thing, you didn't see why you had to, and you didn't remember the old thing. You'd get dizzy and you'd feel bad; in fact, you'd have a right to feel bad. Because though the mind wants new things, and has a right to them, and has a right to change and be different, and all that—still, if there's nothing that puts all these different things together, it's just too bad. All this change will disappoint.

Now in the song I mentioned, there are many different things. The notes change, and so do the words. There isn't so much change as in going from an onion to a clothespin to a book to a person, but there's change.

What is also there in the song? There is something that keeps the notes and words together. Well, when you think of anything which has lots of different things in it and you can see them together—these different things, along with being different, are also the same.

This may be hard. I'll try to explain another way. Take the numbers 2, 4, and 8. These numbers are all different, but they have something the same, because 2 is half of 4 and 4 is half of 8. And 4 is twice 2, and 8 is twice 4. There is a sameness among these numbers then. This sameness is what some people would call "order," too.

If those notes in the song are different, and they go together in some way, just as with the numbers I gave you, there is sameness, too. This may sound awfully strange, but anytime, James, you see some things at one time, with your mind, as different and also as together or the same, you'll be seeing a beautiful thing. This is really why you saw or heard the song as beautiful,

or pretty ("saw" and "heard" here mean the same).

Take a pretty little girl, the girl you know called Cora Hill. Now pretty little girls have been compared to songs before; but did you ever think that you could really, truly, not just in sort of fun, compare a girl to a song? (And Cora, I think, is sensible and kind and bright, and that helps her being pretty.) A person wrote the song and he wanted to make it good, or beautiful. Cora's mother, I think, wanted her to look good; but she didn't have so much to do with it as the person who wrote the song did with the song. (And I like Cora's mother, too.)

As I said, the song consists of notes and chords and such things which are different and yet go together. Now if Cora is pretty, something like this is true, too. She has a nose which is different from her eyes and her mouth, but which seems to go together with these; in fact, one seems to grow out from the other. Then her ears and her hair and her

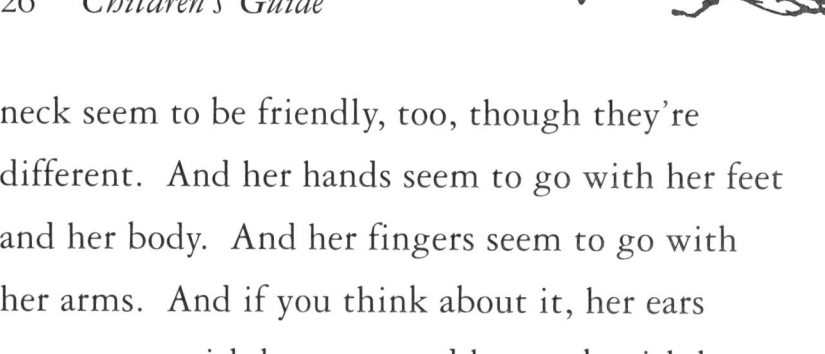

neck seem to be friendly, too, though they're different. And her hands seem to go with her feet and her body. And her fingers seem to go with her arms. And if you think about it, her ears seem to go with her toes, and her neck with her arms, and her eyes with her feet, and her nose with the front of her body; and everything I have mentioned seems to go well with everything else I could mention.

What you have in the good body of Cora are a lot of different things, a lot of change, that don't seem to make for bad jumps and unfriendliness among each other. When many things are so among each other that you feel: "See, they're different, but they seem to be close, too"—then you feel what some people call composition, which has a great, great deal to do with beauty. You could say, all right, there's composition in the song I mentioned and in Cora's body, although the composition came in different ways.

I haven't said all the things that you can find in what's beautiful. Offhand, though, doesn't it seem that if three hundred people see three hundred beautiful things, what happens each time is, in a way, the same? Yes, if you yourself, James, saw three hundred beautiful things—a flower, a tablecloth, a picture, an animal, and so on—if you really saw each as beautiful, then even though the things you saw as beautiful were all different, still what happened in your mind was pretty much the same. If you found what it was which was the same every time you saw what was beautiful, that thing which was the same was *why* a thing was beautiful.

You should think about this a lot. Some miserable people say that when anyone sees what is beautiful, it's only in his mind, and you can never find out what makes an object beautiful. Well, I don't believe this. It's true, beauty happens in your mind, but the feeling that something is beautiful is always a combination of your mind and what it's meeting; and the combination can be looked at; and you can say things about the combination.

Let's take another beautiful thing, a tree. A tree has a trunk, and it has branches and twigs and leaves; and the leaves have things in them, too. You see the tree changing as you look at it, and remaining the same. You see curves and straight lines in the tree, and the curves are like straight lines, and the straight lines are like curves. (Such things happen in Cora's body, too.) Well, when you get the feeling that change is going on—as with curves and straight lines—and it's all part of the same thing, you have movement in what isn't moving; and that makes beauty, too.

I could use other words, but, James, when you feel that something is the same and also changing at *one* time, you're going to feel you're up against something beautiful. In other essays more will be said having to do with this.

3. PEOPLE

People are of all kinds. No matter what kind they are, they have something to do with you. You use people right when, by finding out what they are, you come to be more yourself. Every person can tell you something about yourself.

If you, James Nash, meet a person called Henry Wills, then it should be James Nash plus Henry Wills in such a way that James Nash is more by the addition of or meeting with Henry Wills. This, I think, seems reasonable. But often it isn't that way at all. Somebody called Tom Hale meets Henry Wills; and something in Tom Hale wants to think the existence of Henry Wills is an interference, something that makes Tom Hale less, insults him.

If Tom Hale thinks this way, he doesn't like people. He can smile and be courteous and bring a glass of water to a person and ask persons to visit him, but he doesn't like people. You like people truly when you can truly think they exist to make you more: that is, they exist to make you more when you *know* them, not when, just, you are fooling them and making them do as you want them to do, and are not giving them insides of the sort you give yourself.

The first thing necessary in liking people is to see that they have insides just as you have. In every person, thoughts go on, thoughts about himself and other things. And it is so easy to make oneself important by saying that what goes on in oneself has nothing much to do with other things. This is a way to get a certain kind of importance, but it is also a way to be awfully, sadly, disgustingly lonely. Most

people come to feel lonely in this way—at least partly.

People are wonderful. Just think that each mind which exists is a way all by itself of taking trees into it and mountains and sounds and laughter and pictures and philosophy books and other people. Individuality is wonderful. Individuality is a way one thing has of knowing it's one thing by knowing about everything. People, however, come to think they have individuality by closing their eyes, doing things with other people before they (the people with "individuality") really see the other people. If you start doing things in your mind with people before you see them, you can talk or think about individuality all you want: you won't have it. What you'll have is a cave-like, twisted, dull snobbishness which gives itself fancy names and is afraid: is afraid because at any time it may be found out.

Children should know that to think is wonderful.

One sign of an awful kind of snobbishness is to think that because there is very, very much of something, that something is somehow not so important. This isn't true. If there were a million poems in the world, a poem would still be wonderful. There have been millions of sunrises; but a sunrise is still wonderful. For a thing to be wonderful means for it to be able to give you big, sensible thoughts without your knowing—at least right away—where they came from, or how big they are, or how far they can go.

All people are wonderful, because mind in any person is wonderful. Where people are not wonderful, it's because they aren't sufficiently people: that is, they accept dullness. Dullness in people is of two kinds. Both come from one big, not so good way of mind.

A person is dull when he sees things which should be exciting, are strange, have life, are beautiful, are new, are good, and this person just goes ahead as if nothing had happened. Dullness of this kind is very common. A person is dull when something in that person stops him from being affected by what he should be affected by. This kind of person can look at a sunrise and yawn; can hear a strange, good thing and act like dull ashes in cream; can be in front of a swift, fine thing and go ahead as if he had heard the multiplication table recited for the seventy-sixth time in a row. This kind of dullness comes from a person's being afraid to have something change in himself. So he doesn't want, deep down, to have things affect him with him showing it. Many people think this is a kind of power; but I say, and James Nash should say, the hell with it.

I talk now of the other kind of dullness. This dullness is not so much of how you take things, but of how you show things; or as a learned man in a college might say, how you express yourself. Some people think it's right not to show feeling. They want to imitate regular fish who have no worries. They think that if they screamed or shouted, they'd be losing so much, so much. They like to talk as if they were counting fat pigeons in a dull forest. This sort of dullness comes, as I said, from the same thing as the other kind. It comes from a very deep conceit. I shall explain conceit more, as I go on.

Now, when a person is not wholly a person, he is not giving himself to things and he is not ready to have things act on him. The *people* part of him, the *person* part of him, wants nothing like this conceited dullness. People want to feel things and want to show that what things do to them is good for them, and they're proud of it.

The *people* or *person* side in a human being we can never dislike. If we do, we dislike ourselves.

36 *Children's Guide*

This is not all I'm going to say about people. It hardly is. But since I don't want these essays to be too long, it more than likely is good to stop here.

4. MOTHERS

Cora Hill's mother is sensible. When Cora was born, Selma Hill didn't just think now that Cora was born she had something more important than a new dress or a new car; and she didn't always think "my Cora." Cora's mother knew that the baby Cora came from something much bigger than herself; that she wasn't just a little Selma. When Cora was born, Selma didn't say, "Well, I know what I want her to be like, and since I gave birth to her, I want her to be this way and this way."

Selma was a respectful mother. She felt that even if Cora was tiny, she might be wanting to feel and do various things just because she was Cora, recently arrived from a big, big world with Selma's help. Yes, Selma wanted to find out about Cora. She didn't just say:

"I'm a big person, and I'm going to tell Cora everything." She felt she could learn from Cora, even.

How very few mothers are this way! How very few mothers, say, five feet six inches tall, want to learn from a baby maybe about one foot six inches tall. And Cora's mother didn't learn about her just from books, either; though she did read them. Because if you want to find out about anything, it's a good idea to see what's in books; books can be wonderful in making your mind bigger and able to do more. Cora's mother, though, didn't just see her baby in terms of some of the big words used in the books, and didn't think the books said *everything* about Cora, or for that matter, any other child.

When Cora was growing up, she didn't think her mother was somebody very far away from her some of the time, and at other times was so close to her, did so much for her, that Cora could think this big person was hers, only hers. Cora was able to think that Selma was

the bigger person, yes, but just like her; and Cora was able to think that what she wanted to find out about was also what Selma wanted to find out about, except that Selma began finding out earlier.

And then when Cora was in Selma's arms, she didn't get the feeling that this was all that mattered, and that other people were far off and not like her mother at all. Cora's mother wanted her baby to like her, but she didn't act in such a way it seemed she didn't want Cora to like anyone else. Cora's mother was someone who felt: "I got here first, and without me, you wouldn't have got here. I'm here, though, to tell you about everything so that you will see the more you know about everything the better you'll feel."

And Cora's mother tried for her to understand other little boys and girls and even grownups; and her mother told Cora about cats and about plants and about trains (a little later) and about food and about the sky, and showed how they all were close to Cora, and if she didn't know them and like knowing them, she wouldn't know about herself, either. And Cora's mother said that if she didn't know about herself, she wouldn't be satisfied with herself, because if you think you're satisfied with yourself and you don't know about yourself, you're really satisfied with somebody else.

Cora's mother was so sensible, I wouldn't blame anybody if he thought she didn't exist. It's very good to know about her though.

The mother of Delia Hanson you can see very often. Oh, she read the books, all right. But the books didn't change her. When Delia was born, Priscilla Hanson thought, here was a way of fighting some of the things she didn't like in her husband, Roger.

Delia Hanson's mother thought, just so, that Delia was better than all other children, just because she was born to Priscilla. Priscilla Hanson thought her baby was hers, the way a rug from Persia might be. She wouldn't put it that way, but that's the way she felt.

The books told her that Delia should be dealt with like an "individual"; but the books never made it really clear for Priscilla what an "individual" was. Priscilla Hanson thought too much about just herself and her family; and the books didn't stop her from that. The books went around in Priscilla's mind, but they never got very far. Maybe they could have: anyway, they didn't.

Delia came to think very early she was something very special. She saw Priscilla sometimes cry; and she knew it was about Roger. Delia also knew that Priscilla took her on her lap just because it made her feel better when Roger seemed mean. And Priscilla once held Delia close, close to her and said: "You, dear, are the only thing I really care for." Wasn't it awful that the books didn't stop Priscilla from saying such things?

And then Priscilla would go out with her friends, and it didn't seem to be the Priscilla who held Delia close, close to her. This Priscilla seemed somebody else. The books, too, didn't stop Priscilla from seeming somebody else.

Delia got to feeling that Priscilla was kind of fooling her. She liked the nice things her mother did for her, but she wasn't sure it was all Priscilla. Delia came to feel grownups fooled little children, and weren't so smart, and had to be fooled themselves.

There are many, many mothers in America. I'm going to say more about them. Right now, it's right to say, most of them are too much like Delia's mother.

BIG QUESTIONS FOR LITTLE ONES

1. Would you like to be a mystery to your mother, or do you want her to know you more and more?

2. Is there any way that your mother is smarter than you?

3. Is it well to think a lot of your mother or not?

4. Do you like yourself for how you see your mother?

5. Do you like yourself for how you see people?

6. Do you want your mother to see you in a way completely different from the way she sees other people, including Dad?

7. Do you want your father and mother to get along, or do you want them to be in a state of disagreement?

8. Can you use your mother to see everything better?

9. What do you think your mother was like at your age?

10. What is the most useful thing you could say to your mother?

11. When you were sarcastic with your mother (if you were), did it do you any good?

12. Do you feel your mother has a right to think about you and do herself good by thinking about you?

13. Where are your thoughts like those of your mother?

14. If you don't do all you can to make your mother stronger and happier, will you be against yourself or not?

Mr. Siegel wrote these questions in 1973, with the following note:
Dedicated to Aesthetic Realism consultants and consultations, present and future.

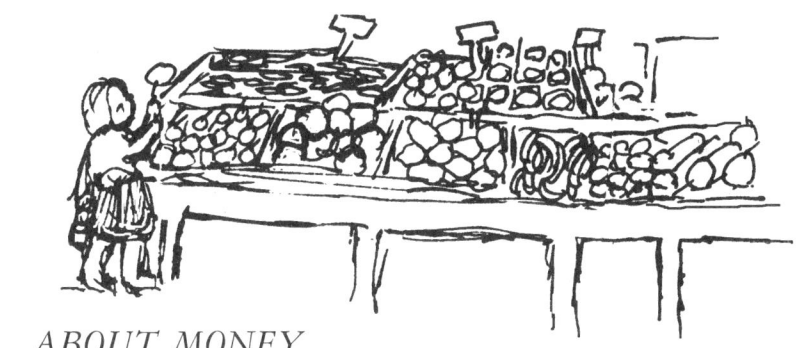

5. ABOUT MONEY

Money is what you buy things with, and that means a great deal; for everybody has to do with things. When you buy a thing, that thing is supposed to be yours, and that means a great deal, too. One of the meanings of these words: "It's yours," is that you can do what you want with it. So money lets you have things that you can do what you want with.

What are some of the things money can let you have? Suppose Delia Hanson, of whom I've already written, buys a dress, or has her mother buy it for her. Then she can do what she wants (including, of course, wear it) with the dress money has bought. —If she can't do what she wants with it, it isn't wholly hers.

Now what about this dress? No one ever yet saw a dress grow on a tree, or in a field, or come down from the sky ready to be worn. The things in the dress did come from the ground—the dress is of cotton. There is a little belt on the dress and it has a little buckle that came from metal also coming from the ground. Then there is a nice yellow and green coloring to the dress, and that came from what smart people call chemicals, which, like the cotton, also came from the ground.

Still, as Delia and you know, that isn't the whole dress. The dress has sleeves, and sleeves don't grow from the ground; and the cotton you see in Georgia maybe in the moving pictures, or maybe in Georgia, isn't just the cotton you have in Delia's dress. Then the dress fits Delia, and the fit didn't come out of the ground, either. When Delia bought the dress, she bought all the things like cotton, metal, coloring in the dress, and also what was done about the cotton, metal, and coloring. She surely bought a whole lot.

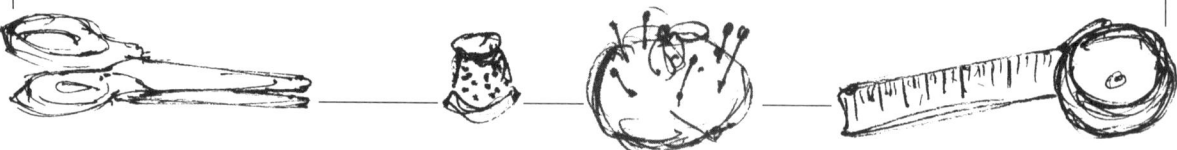

Well, Delia may not think about it, but she's buying what other people have done; in fact, she's buying the time, the work, and the life, up to a point, of other people. This may sound funny, but Delia has to deserve having the cotton, metal, and coloring which come from the ground; and the time, the work, and the life of other people—people most likely she never heard of.

Delia hasn't thought of these things when buying a dress; and many other people haven't thought of these things, either. Yet why shouldn't we deserve it when we start thinking that we can do what we please with something which has in it the time, the work, the life of other people—maybe even the pain?

When we have money, we are able to buy something of the lives of other people. Money is a way of having for ourselves objects which couldn't have been if it wasn't either for the ground—that is, nature—or for what other people have done. Plainly, if we get what other people made, we have to think we have a right to it. The first step in having a right to what other people have made is to think about it.

Money is wonderful (and it isn't the only thing that's wonderful). Just think: it can buy pigs and books and grass by the yard and tablecloths and theatre tickets and sugar and old books and songs and cheese and music—and what else, what else? You could never stop mentioning the things money can get for you, or somebody else. Money stands for all the things I have written down and many, many more. They all are either ground or people's work, or both. Now Delia never made the ground, so she and nobody else has any special claims to it; and she never made other people (even if she grows up and has a child, she doesn't make people just like that).

Yet she feels when she buys things, "They are mine." Why? What does this mean? How can they be really hers; how can she deserve them? The children of America and grownups should think about this. If they do, they will be thinking about money. When you know what is really yours and why it ought to be, you've gone pretty far towards being what you ought to be; which is all the time what you truly want to be.

6. OBJECTS

Objects are what you have around you when you're born and much later. Even when you die, you have objects around you. You should be glad of this. Many people, without knowing it, are not glad when they have objects around them. They don't like them.

You, James, are thinking of something right now. It's an object. You can say "you" to yourself and also "that." As "that" has something done to it by you, it's an object. Anything which you can see as having something done to it by you, is an object.

When, however, you do something to something else, that thing does something to you, too. This is what is going to happen to you all your life. All your life can be seen as made up of three Somethings: You, Something

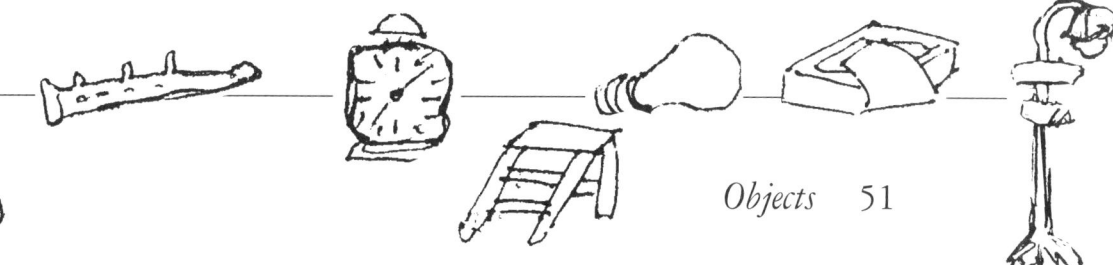

Else, and the Something that goes on between you and the Something Else.

If you're happy, these three Somethings will be well arranged. The arrangement will be beautiful.

It should be clear that if you're happy, it's going to be something which will make you happy. Ask yourself this: When you were happy some time ago (I'm assuming you were), what was it which made you happy?

You were happy either because you made yourself happy or because something else did or because both you and something else did. Now if it was you, yourself, that made yourself happy, why can't you do this all the time? Did something enable you to make yourself happy at one time and stop you at another? You, yourself, surely, if you were doing all this alone, would have kept on being happy all the time.

You wanted to be happy all the time, didn't you? So, again, what stopped you? It was either something in yourself or something not in yourself; that is, outside

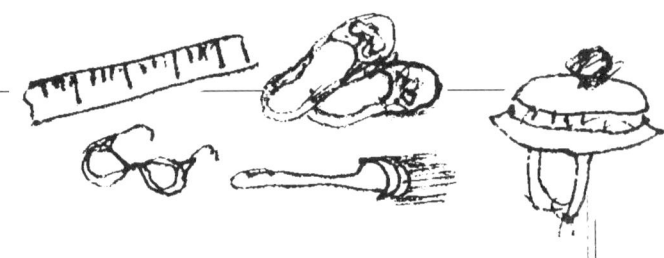

of you. If it was the first, why should you, yourself, stop yourself from being happy? If it was the second, then something else could affect you so much it could stop you from being happy. Now this thing which stopped you from being happy (if it did) is an object as soon as you start thinking about it. If something besides you, outside of you, enabled you to be happy, this, too, is an object once you start thinking about it.

The thing that makes you go, makes you happy or unhappy, is thought about by you even when you don't know it. Since it does so much to you, it surely is a big object. This object of objects is Everything, the World, What's Real.

You can, if you want, think about anything in What's Real; and as soon as you do, it is an object.

All this shows that objects are important. You have to think about them, and you do.

7. FEELING BAD

When you feel bad it is a good thing to know why. Very many people don't know why. They even want to think there is no reason why. But there is.

If you feel bad, then you're in some arrangement with things (including the things in yourself) which isn't correct. At every moment in your life, you're in some arrangement with things.

At any moment, too, you have some opinion about things. You think they're either good or bad. Thinking a thing is either good or bad is having an opinion about it. Children have opinions just as much as grownups do.

Now a person can think that a cake is good and he himself is bad; or he can think a cake is bad and he himself is good; or he can think (lucky fellow) that both he and the cake are good.

People want to think that things are good. They also want to think that they themselves are good. But sometimes a person can think he is good just because something else is bad. This person whom we can call Ted may even think he feels good just because he can see something else as bad and can think he's better than that thing. If he does this, Ted won't feel good about the way he feels good. Something in him he may not know very much about will tell him: "This is no way of feeling good, Ted."

So we come to one way of feeling bad that is hard to get at. This is the way by which you feel good just because you have an opinion something else is bad. And something in you may want, even, that things be bad so you can say you're good. If a boy grows up hoping without knowing it that things around him—say, his father and mother—be bad so he can think *he's* good, he is going to be nervous; that is, he'll want things around

Feeling Bad   55

him to be good but also not want them to be good, because when they're bad he can think he's awfully big.

Anyway, when you feel bad, it's either because something in you is not working well with something else in you, or because you are not working well with things around you. If things around you make you feel bad, then you'll be in a way happy, because you'll know that the more you know about those things in What's Real, the less unhappy they'll make you. This happens only, however, when something in you doesn't hope *in the least* that they be bad. Because, you see, one thing in us gets pleasure from the world when we see it as good, and the other thing in us gets pleasure when we see the world as bad. You see, we can say then: "Look at that. I'm better than all that; I have something in me that is better for me than all that, and I can get away from it." The person saying this means by "that" the world. How bad.

People don't feel good when they're not getting

along with other things and themselves. Offhand, it would seem that if the world made both Ted and all other things, there would be no reason for a serious quarrel. But quarrels there are.

The quarrels, though, come from the fact that there are two Teds. The job ahead of Ted is to make the two things in himself work like one thing, just as a pair of scissors does, or two lines meeting in a point of a triangle. You can look at a triangle about here.

One part of Ted is nothing but Ted. After all, Ted has his own body. When he's in the rain, it is he that feels the rain. It is hard to describe just what Ted feels about himself. But we all know what this feeling is. It is so warm, so right there, so hard to think it isn't. It is true nobody knows the way you feel as you do. Yet although there is this awfully big and warm and strange You feeling, still one can ask: "Where did I come from, and what do I need to be me?"

Everybody needed something to come from. When

you think of what you come from, you'll never stop. It doesn't end with your mother, you know. She had a lot to come from, too. What you come from is also what you're going to get things out of if you're happy. Ted (who may be you, James Nash, when you're not so good) is really not alone, even if he feels like being: he's in an arrangement with what he came from and what he's going to get things out of. Each of these things having so much to do with Ted, is the world.

When Ted feels bad he is in some not so good arrangement with his big, big, big partner. How a bad arrangement like this takes place, I'll take up later. Anyway, when you feel bad, look at yourself and everything, everything, everything that isn't yourself; first you, then everything, then both at once.

8. HAPPENINGS

Happenings are what are taking place all the time. Whenever you change, something has happened. A happening is a motion which you have to think about—it means so much to you.

Getting out of bed each morning you don't see as a happening, because you don't see it as something special. You see it as something that just has to be. So you don't tell someone, "Something happened today: I got out of bed this morning." But if you had been sick for some weeks, and you had been lying in bed day after day, when you did get out of bed one morning and stayed out, that would have been a happening.

Seeing a leaf in a morning is not a happening, because you think seeing a leaf is pretty much of an ordinary bit of life. But if you saw a leaf in such a way it would mean much, much to you, that would be a happening. In fact, a good question at this point is, Why can't you see a leaf in such a way as to make it a happening?

Life—and that takes in a little boy's life—consists, as most people see it, of a lot of ordinary business interrupted by happenings. Happenings are what surprise or excite you: everything else you have to go through (you think to yourself) just because you're alive. A happening is something new. What isn't a happening is old stuff. —So your life is made up of what you can expect, or at least what doesn't surprise you, and what makes you take notice.

Now two kinds of things are going on: the kind of thing which makes you wish for something new to take place, and the kind of thing that makes you think you want some rest. People can not like their lives or what they're doing for two reasons: one, because they're

always doing the same thing with no surprises; and two, because they don't know where they are, so many things are taking place. People all over the world are looking for either excitement or rest; or to use other words, adventure or security.

When people have excitement, they will say they're having lots of "happenings"; when they have rest or security, it's pretty hard to see the happenings. The truth, James, is that you have to have the feeling of rest and excitement all the time. If you have one and are looking for the other, you won't like the one you have very much. The way to get the feeling of rest and adventure at one time is to see "happenings" in what's new and what's old. You may not know it, but if you look hard enough, you can find newness or excitement in what is going on every hour and every day.

You don't have to wait till you're sick to see that getting out of bed can be a big "happening." You don't have to wait till you haven't eaten for three days to find eating some bread and butter pretty exciting. You can find the surprising in many more places than people know usually.

9. BEING ANGRY

Everybody gets angry now and then. We don't have to, though. And when one is angry, as when one is something else, there is a reason.

Anger is a feeling. Every feeling has in it pleasure or pain. I suppose everybody would say that anger is pain rather than pleasure. But anger is not like the pain, just so, of having walked too much and being tired, or worrying about whether someone will get well, or not having had food for a long time. Anger can be close to the things I've just mentioned, but it does seem different.

So what kind of pain is anger, and where does it come from? We are hungry if we haven't had food for many hours, but as I said, we don't have to be angry because of this. What would make us angry?

Well, we'd be angry if along with being hungry, we knew that somebody was trying to stop us from eating by holding food from us, keeping us locked up so we couldn't get food, or even not wanting to sell it to us. In each instance of this not having food, there would be hunger, but also something else, which it seems right to call anger.

It is clear that there have been two kinds of pain: one coming from hunger, which is surely something a person doesn't want ordinarily; and the other coming from having been dealt with in a way one doesn't like. In other words, when we feel that a person has given us pain in a way we don't like, or see as deserved, we are angry. The big question comes up, Why do we think we don't like the way we are dealt with, or don't think we deserve what we are getting or not getting from people?

You can be angry in a good way. If somebody tells a lie about you, and you know you don't deserve it, then the person telling the lie has done an ugly thing; and you have a right to stop people from doing ugly things. One way of having people stop doing ugly things is to make it clear to these people that they will have pain by doing these things. If these people think they have pleasure doing ugly things (and many people do), it is right to teach them that being mean, for example, shouldn't make for fun.

It is hard being angry in the right way. When we are not angry in the right way, something in us knows we are wrong, and we don't like ourselves for it. To be angry in the right way is better than to be pleased in the wrong way.

When we try to stop a person from doing ugly things, we are really trying to make him stronger. So even if we're angry with a person, and the anger is good, we are for the strength of that person. We can criticize him very much, but the criticism goes after something good.

But there is also an anger which comes from thinking too much of ourselves; an anger which comes from conceit. Let's say someone says something true about us. We have in ourselves a nice picture of what we are. So we don't like to hear this thing which interferes with this nice picture. "My, that he can say such things about *me!*" something in us says (quite foolishly).

Suppose Delia Hanson is angry because something has been said of her which is true but which she didn't want to hear. She can think then that Dave Hall, who said this thing, was mean and was against her, and she had to do something against him, because in doing something against him, she would feel she had really made out Dave as bad on this point. She may also not only have something against Dave, but even against her little sister, Helen; because if Dave, who said something against her and made her feel bad, was someone who was outside of her, then Delia could say in her mind:

"Dave is not myself. *I* wouldn't say such mean things myself to myself. Only what was not myself, not Delia, could be so awful." So if Delia thinks that Dave stands for what isn't herself, and can do mean things, then Helen, her little sister, who also can stand for what isn't herself, can do mean things, too.

I know this is a little hard, but whenever we don't like the way something which isn't just ourselves acts towards us, we can sort of take it out on *everything* which isn't ourselves. This means that if Delia thinks she's been insulted by Dave, she can say something mean to Helen. Or, she also might use Helen against Dave. Anyway, Delia is not being angry in a good way.

The first thing in being angry is to find out just what you're being angry about. Delia, for instance, wasn't so angry with what Dave Hall said. You really can't be angry with anything that tells you what's true about you. Delia was angry because if she found out what was true in Dave's words, she would be feeling not so comfortable, so nice. She was wrong, but little girls, like grownups, can be this way. So Delia had to give up a notion about herself, or think Dave and everything like him was just bad.

Delia was saying, "Unhappiness, come on," when she didn't want to find out just what was so or not so about herself. Because when you have a notion about yourself, and you don't want to find out just what you really are, you are ashamed deep, deep down; you know you don't have what you really are, and you don't like it. In fact, you are angry with yourself for not being what you really are and not very much wanting to be.

Delia was one of those people who felt it was nice to think she was all right just by making pictures of herself in herself. She also knew these pictures weren't real, just like that. But she didn't want to give up those pictures. She had to hide, too, to keep on having them. This made her feel that the things she hid from didn't like her, were not on her side. So not being able to do much about the way she was ashamed of herself, or angry with herself, she was angry with other things.

If she could really feel that Dave could tell her something about herself in the same way she could, she would have listened in a different way to him. But when Delia listens to people, she wants to hear all kinds of things in advance. This makes it so that when other people talk, Delia often hears something too different from what she hears when she talks to herself. So, since other things often tell her something against what she tells herself, it isn't too much to say that Delia is angry with things, just as things, except when they talk the same way she talks to herself. She was angry with Dave Hall because Dave made it clear that maybe she had to hear what other things were saying. Poor Delia.

This isn't all about being angry. I will say much more

when I talk of other things. One thing I tell you now: It doesn't pay to be angry with things that aren't you; that is, the world. If you don't see the world as your friend, it will be poor James Nash, just as I said, Poor Delia.

10. WORK

All people work. Work is beginning with something and ending with something that you want and other people may want. A fine instance of work—there are many others—is the chair. You don't see animals sitting on chairs, unless they've first been made by men. When first chairs were made, somebody felt he'd get along better if besides walking, running, and lying on the grass or elsewhere, or sitting on the grass or elsewhere, he'd sit on something between him and the ground.

The earliest people alive—whoever they were—got along without chairs. Chairs were made for people living much later—for example, ourselves. Somebody or some people worked to get to chairs; and have them.

One thing necessary in work is a feeling of what you want. All work is a way of getting what people want. Suppose you started (and you, here, are likely a girl) with some cloth, and you wanted a little bag from the cloth. So looking at the cloth, you'd think of the bag. Then you would take scissors and a needle, or maybe do some measuring; and using scissors and needle and cloth and your hands for some time—all the while knowing you wanted to have a bag—you would, after a while, come to have a bag. You would have worked; you would have known what you wanted; and you would have got what you had in your mind. Maybe you could even give the bag as a present to another little girl. A bag could have been a want of hers, too.

Work is a way of doing as we want to do. I said that all people work. By this I mean that if you see a chair in one end of a room, and you know you have to walk to the end of the room to get to the chair and sit in it, and

you do walk to the end of the room, you have been working. You have used your body in order to get something you wanted.

Suppose there was an old lady in a room who was tired, and you, James Nash, knew where a chair was. So you went into the room where the chair was, and brought the chair to where the old lady was. The old lady might smile and say, "Here's a dime for you, my boy." So you would be paid for your work; but it would have been work whether you were paid for it or not.

All work, James, has to do with pleasure. Pleasure is what goes with things when you want these things to go on; or, if you like, not to stop. Whether we know it or not, like it or not, we go after pleasure. When a person goes towards a chair to sit down, he thinks he'd like it better being in a chair than standing up. So he takes a little walk in order to feel better than he did. This walk, as I have said, is really work.

All work is for something. If you think the heart in your body is beating for something, it is working. If you even are sleeping in order to do something later, you are working. As soon as anything one does is looked on as being for something, it is work.

Still, work is given a much smaller meaning. People mostly think they work when they go to a factory or office, and stop playing or sleeping or talking; and later get paid by a man in the factory or office. This idea of work isn't so good. I say this because the chief thing in work is its being useful. Surely, if what people call play is useful, and what they may call work—which they may get paid for—is not useful, then play is more work than "work."

It is necessary, James, to know what you want and to do things for what you want, before you are working clearly. If people thought more of what gave pleasure or did good or was useful, instead of where things were done and how they were paid for, these people would

74   *Children's Guide*

know better what work is. A baby, as soon as it's born, is working in order to live. To do anything that is truly *good* for ourselves or others is work. This will become clearer in other essays.

11. BOOKS

Books are a way of learning about the world without having to do the things you have to do when you learn about the world in other ways. Everything tells you about the world, which is Everything; but books are a special way of telling you.

    A little boy can think of what happened two hundred years ago; and he can be happy, and more himself, doing so. And ask yourself, where are you going to learn about how people felt long ago unless you go to books? And if there's some strange place, a book can tell you of it, even though you may go to this place later.

    Do you know, James, that all your feelings could be put into a book and printed in thousands of copies? What's more, your feelings, if truly written about, would be of value to ever so many people; there's really no limit to the number of people who could get something important for themselves in reading about the feelings of James Nash. You can have things happen inside you by reading about Indians or Englishmen or brave women or forests or crowds of people long ago; and all these look quite strange to you; but if the feelings you had this morning, James, and at all other times, were described, put in a book, people might think, "How strange all this is." Still, if the book were written truly and rightly, your feelings would be added to their feelings.

That's what books do: they add feelings to other feelings. Every time you read a book, someone else's feelings meet yours, and mix with yours. You are always being affected by other people's feelings; but books are the big way of bringing to a person the feelings he might never have otherwise.

Only in a book can you feel America all at once and in some detail. A person has feelings, and he knows a

lot about America, and he writes his feelings down; and he says to other persons, "Come, let your feelings meet mine; if they do, good things will happen." If he doesn't believe this, he shouldn't write a book.

Can you think of anything, James, that can't get into a book? Now lots of things haven't got into books, but that doesn't mean they can't or shouldn't. People are likely any day to get new thoughts or happenings into a book.

If you read a book about the sea, it can go pretty far in making you feel the mist on the water, the motion of the ship, the dark look of the sky, the wind that soon may be rising, the deck, and what's underneath the deck. I'm thinking now of a ship in the Pacific about 1780. How awful it would be if no one could read about the way ships were in the Pacific in the year 1780! You may never have missed this before, or thought of missing it: but, James, how would you feel if you knew 1780 and ships on the Pacific in twilight in 1780 could never,

never be written about; never, never be put in a book; never, never be felt in print? You'd say, "How very bad." It is good that ships on the Pacific in 1780 need never be forgot, can be thought about, can be felt.

Then there can be books about cities and little girls and old women and electricity and the future and love and you (there can be such a book) and worries and love again and America and all your friends. All these books would consist of words. Words are a way of feeling things without having those things under your nose. Words put together can tell you about the world no end. Even a bad book tells you about the world. It may not do right to the world, but in it you can find out about the world anyway. You just have to use your time the best way.

Some people can't read books. It's likely that people who can't read books can't have their feelings affected much by other persons, either, and, for that matter, by things generally. These people think that they

have "themselves," so why do they have to read books very deeply? They are wrong, because if they know how to read books, their "selves" are a lot more. Many of these people don't know they don't like really to read books. They don't like to, though. When they do read, it's not because they want their feelings to be affected by other feelings, but because they can seem important to themselves and other people. They don't give themselves to print; they let print do something to their minds, but they don't let print go very deep. That would mean other people's feelings were allowed to be like their own.

Books tell us really the same kind of thing that walking on the street does. We feel and learn when we walk on the street; we also feel and learn when we read books. We want things to happen to our minds. When we read books our minds "go out" more, work more, to have things happen to us. Therefore, if we can't read books, we don't like life, either. This is so because life in its widest form and its deepest comes to a person when he

80   *Children's Guide*

is able to feel life through words. Words, when they're good, don't make life duller; not at all. They show how life is good and great because it can have excitement while it is spoken of more truly than is the usual case. Books can show that life can make sense, while it makes you wonder, and think, and hope, and see what is right under your feet.

12. THE WORLD

I have just now written of Books, which are a way of getting the world and all its feelings into print. So what is this world I'm always talking about and don't want to forget? You feel, James, that something exists. You know a floor is under you, and there is air around your ear. And you know your mother and father exist; and you know those two different girls, Cora Hill and Delia Hanson, exist. Everything I mentioned can do something to you; you can hide all you want, but you know they can do something to you. One way of describing the world is: Everything that can do something to you.

Do you know everything that can do something to you? You don't, and no one does. Still, you must be interested in what can do something to you, even if you don't know what it is. Because, it is pretty clear, if you're not interested in what can do something to you, you can hardly be said to be interested in yourself.

Now things can do something to you in various ways. The moon can make you think about it; the wind can blow on you; well cooked meat can make you feel good when you eat it; a little girl can touch your hand, and make you think she's nice because she does this; your mother can scold you; and a noise can frighten or worry you. I've given you some samples of how the world does things to you, but there are so many, so many more, that if I began to count or list them, you can think of yourself as growing I don't know how many beards reaching to the floor before I was through. And yet, James, all the things I could count or list, while those beards were growing, would affect you.

Do you know anything you can't think of? You don't. The question itself seems silly. Still, when you think of anything at all, something happens to

you, because the thing you think of becomes part of your mind. Try it. Think of a green bird flying over a square mile of ice in the northernmost Pacific. Well, you may never see this green bird, or even the ice, but they're in your mind; and in a way, they'll never get out of it. You may think you forget, but all that means is that the James Nash who remembers and talks in the afternoon, can't remember; but there is a James Nash that doesn't remember and talk, it just remembers and never talks; but it doesn't forget, because what happened is still around.

So think of a big meal in the year 1020, about 925 years ago.* You have to admit that if the year 1945—or this year—exists, there's a chance that the year 1020 existed, too. It is hard to think that the year 1020 existed just as much as this year does, but it did. People don't want at all to think that something happened *really* in 1020. But though it may not make these people comfortable, 1020 had lots of happenings like

---
*Mr. Siegel wrote this in 1945.

happenings that are going to take place tomorrow.

No matter how far you go back in time, it's still the world, and it still can do things to you. What happens to you when you think of the year 476? You may say, What have I got to do with this? But do you feel bigger or smaller when you think of a cat in 476, or a fire or a smile or a joke or another little boy in this same year? When you think of the subjects I have mentioned, don't you feel bigger? You may feel strange, but don't you feel bigger?

I have given you some idea of what the world is. It can go as far back in time as you please, and can also go wherever you want in the space around you. As soon as you think something is *anywhere,* that's the world. The world is your partner, whatever your mind may do. The world makes funny stories, lightning, mothers, balls, picnics, spears—and here, if I go on, once again I say you could grow many beards going to the floor before I'd be through.

James, wherever you are, in bed or out, the world will be about you. If you get along well with it, you will be *some* citizen. That's the job. Every other job is part of this one.

BOOKS BY ELI SIEGEL

Self and World: An Explanation of Aesthetic Realism

Hot Afternoons Have Been in Montana: Poems
  With a Letter by William Carlos Williams

Hail, American Development (Poems)

*James and the Children: A Consideration of Henry James's
  "The Turn of the Screw"*

The Modern Quarterly *Beginnings of
  Aesthetic Realism, 1922-1923*

BOOKS ABOUT ELI SIEGEL AND AESTHETIC REALISM

The Williams-Siegel Documentary
    Ed. Martha Baird and Ellen Reiss

*Aesthetic Realism: We Have Been There
  Six Artists on the Siegel Theory of Opposites*
    Chaim Koppelman et al.

BIOGRAPHICAL NOTES

ELI SIEGEL (1902–1978), poet, critic, philosopher, educator, grew up in Baltimore, Maryland. He became famous in 1925 when his poem "Hot Afternoons Have Been in Montana" won the esteemed *Nation* Poetry Prize. The poet William Carlos Williams was to write years later: "I say definitely that that single poem, out of a thousand others written in the past quarter century, secures our place in the cultural world."

Mr. Siegel founded and began to teach the philosophy Aesthetic Realism in 1941, in New York City. In the decades that followed, he gave thousands of lectures on poetry, history, economics—all the arts and sciences. And he gave thousands of individual lessons to men, women, and children, which taught a new way of seeing the world based on this principle: *"The world, art, and self explain each other: each is the aesthetic oneness of opposites."*

In a Proclamation honoring Mr. Siegel's centenary and designating his hundredth birthday "Eli Siegel Day" in Baltimore, that city's mayor, Martin O'Malley, wrote of "the honesty, kindness, and greatness of mind Eli Siegel possessed," "his scholarship and historic comprehension," and "the classes he taught which changed people's lives magnificently." And Mayor O'Malley wrote:

> This education he founded, enabling people to see the world and others with the respect and kindness they deserve, including people of different races and nationalities, is continued by Class Chairman Ellen Reiss and the faculty of the not-for-profit Aesthetic Realism Foundation, and is used as a Teaching Method with unprecedented success by educators in public schools.

DOROTHY KOPPELMAN is both an artist and an Aesthetic Realism Consultant. Her work has been shown in museums throughout America, including New York's Museum of Modern Art, and is in the collection of the National Museum of Women in the Arts (Washington, DC). In 1955 she founded the Terrain Gallery, which is based on Eli Siegel's landmark principle *"In reality opposites are one; art shows this."* Mrs. Koppelman has taught art at the National Academy of Design, and to children at Brooklyn College. And she teaches "Critical Inquiry: A Workshop in the Visual Arts" at the Aesthetic Realism Foundation. Her drawings in the *Children's Guide* have in them her love for these essays.

ELLEN REISS is the Class Chairman of Aesthetic Realism, appointed by Eli Siegel. A critic and poet, she teaches the professional classes for Aesthetic Realism Consultants and Associates, as well as the course "The Aesthetic Realism Explanation of Poetry," at the Aesthetic Realism Foundation. Prior to becoming Class Chairman, she taught in the English departments of Hunter College and Queens College of the City University of New York. As Editor of the international periodical *The Right of Aesthetic Realism to Be Known,* her commentaries on current events, literature, history, and the human self have been educating people worldwide, and she is considered by many people the foremost educator in the world today.

BEARDSLEY & MEMORIAL LIBRARY

T 83126

BEARDSLEY & MEMORIAL LIBRARY
3 3750 000052431

J814.54 SIEGEL
gel, Eli

UG 2 1 2003
22/12